ULTIMATE NBA Road Trip

By Tyler Mason

ULTIMATE SPORTS
ROAD TRIPS

SportsZone
An Imprint of Abdo Publishing
abdobooks.com

ABDOBOOKS.COM

Published by Abdo Publishing, a division of ABDO, PO Box 398166, Minneapolis, Minnesota 55439.

Printed in the United States of America, North Mankato, Minnesota
092018
012019

Cover Photo: Michael Conroy/AP Images
Interior Photos: Michael Conroy/AP Images, 1; Eric Gay/AP Images, 4–5; Adam Glanzman/Getty Images Sport/Getty Images, 7; Erick W. Rasco/Sports Illustrated/Getty Images, 8; Bruce Bennett/Getty Images Sport/Getty Images, 11; Walter Iooss Jr./Sports Illustrated/Getty Images 12; Frank Franklin II/AP Images, 14–15; Torontonian/Alamy, 17; Warren Toda/EPA/Rex Features, 18; Lance King/Getty Images Sport/Getty Images, 21; Doug McSchooler/AP Images, 22; Jeff Roberson/AP Images, 25; David Banks/AP Images, 26; Andre Jenny Stock Connection Worldwide/Newscom, 29, 44; iStockphoto, 31; Greg Nelson/Sports Illustrated/Getty Images, 32; Uli Deck/picture-alliance/dpa/AP Images, 35; Matt A. Brown/AP Images, 37; Ric Tapia/Icon Sportswire, 38–39, 45; Shutterstock Images, 41; Craig Mitchelldyer/AP Images, 42

Editor: Bradley Cole
Series Designer: Melissa Martin

Library of Congress Control Number: 2018949191

Publisher's Cataloging-in-Publication Data

Names: Mason, Tyler, author.
Title: Ultimate NBA road trip / by Tyler Mason.
Description: Minneapolis, Minnesota : Abdo Publishing, 2019 | Series: Ultimate sports road trips | Includes online resources and index.
Identifiers: ISBN 9781532117541 (lib. bdg.) | ISBN 9781532170409 (ebook)
Subjects: LCSH: Sports arenas--Juvenile literature. | Sports spectators--Juvenile literature. | Basketball--Juvenile literature. | National Basketball Association--Juvenile literature.
Classification: DDC 796.323068--dc23

TABLE OF CONTENTS

Tip-Off!

The ultimate road trip through the National Basketball Association (NBA) will visit arenas throughout the United States and Canada. It will drop in on clubs designed by Drake and courts that have seen championship runs. History will hang from the rafters. Facial recognition protects locker rooms. Arenas will host concerts by the biggest music artists then install the court and change the seats to hold a basketball game the next day.

The road trip will stop in New York, Dallas, Chicago, Portland, Boston, Toronto, Indianapolis, and Los Angeles. It will visit the only fieldhouse in professional

sports in Indianapolis. Los Angeles and New York are big sports cities and the fans show it. Portland is smaller but loves its team fiercely. The atmosphere, fans, history, and amenities make these eight arenas the best places to watch NBA games.

Fans, history, playoff runs, and great plays all make NBA arenas awesome places to visit and catch a game.

TD GARDEN

The original home of the Boston Celtics held lots of history. The Celtics dynasty won 16 championships while playing at Boston Garden. The team wanted to bring parts of that history to its new home in more than just a symbolic fashion. It installed Boston Garden's famous court in the new TD Garden. The floor pattern, known as parquet, is the only one like it in the NBA. Celtics legends such as Larry Bird and Bill Russell played on that court. The flooring was replaced in 2015 during a renovation. Of course the new wood court has the same parquet design.

FUN FACT

TD Garden has hosted the National Collegiate Athletic Association (NCAA) basketball tournament several times. The Celtics' and Bruins' championship banners hanging from the rafters are temporarily removed during the tournament.

For a relatively new building, a lot of history hangs from the rafters of TD Garden. Fans will quickly notice the 23 banners

TD GARDEN

Boston, Massachusetts

Date Opened: September 30, 1995
Capacity: 18,624
Home Team: Boston Celtics

hanging above the court. Seventeen of those celebrate the Celtics' NBA championships. The Boston Bruins of the National Hockey League (NHL), who share the arena, earned the other six titles.

History is important at TD Garden. But in 2014, the arena was given a modern makeover during a renovation. More technology

The Boston Celtics have had plenty of success in TD Garden.

was also installed during the renovation. That included digital touch-screen directories and enhanced wireless internet service. The concourses were updated, too. If fans want a sit-down restaurant experience, they even have three options: Banners Harbor View, Legends, and Premium Club Bistro. More than a dozen new items were added to the concessions.

FUN FACT

TD Garden was originally called Fleet Center when it opened in 1995. The name changed to TD Garden in 2005. The naming rights to the building cost $6 million per year.

More renovations are taking place at TD Garden. An area called the Hub on Causeway will add shops, hotels, and a new entrance to the arena.

Fans who visit TD Garden should catch a tour at the Sports Museum. Located inside the arena on levels 5 and 6, the exhibit showcases items from Boston sports history. The museum is open to the public most days of the year for tours.

And located at 100 Legends Way in Boston, the arena is only a few minutes' walk from the Charles River. Fans riding Boston's train can be dropped off feet away from TD Garden at North Station.

2 MADISON SQUARE GARDEN

Willis Reed made only two baskets in Game 7 of the 1970 NBA Finals. But they might have been the most famous baskets in the history of Madison Square Garden.

Reed injured his leg in Game 5 of the Finals and missed Game 6. It looked like he might miss Game 7 as well. The New York Knicks star did not take the court with his teammates for warm-ups. Then all of a sudden, he hobbled out from the locker room. Willis went through the tunnel to the court for the end of warm-ups just before the game started. The fans at Madison Square Garden erupted. The Knicks went on to win that game against the Los Angeles Lakers for their first NBA title.

FUN FACT

With the Chase Center replacing Oracle Arena in 2019, Madison Square Garden is the oldest arena in the NBA.

MADISON SQUARE GARDEN

New York City, New York

Date Opened: February 11, 1968
Capacity: 19,812
Home Team: New York Knicks

That was only one of the many big moments at the world's most famous arena. Madison Square Garden is one of the most iconic venues in all of sports. The arena is located in the borough of Manhattan in the heart of New York City. It has been the home of the New York Knicks for decades.

But the current Madison Square Garden is not the original arena. There have been four versions of it. The first one opened

Willis Reed (19) was one of many players who helped make the Garden a special place for Knicks fans.

in 1874 and cost $35,000. It was used for social gatherings and exhibits.

The Knicks didn't play at Madison Square Garden until the third edition of the arena, which opened in 1925. The Knicks first played there in 1946. That arena was eventually demolished in 1968. The current Madison Square Garden was completed that same year. The Knicks were not the first basketball team to use the new arena. The Garden first hosted a double header between the Celtics and Detroit Pistons on February 14, 1968.

FUN FACT

Many famous musicians have performed concerts at Madison Square Garden. Some of the most notable acts include Elvis Presley, Michael Jackson, Madonna, and Taylor Swift.

Madison Square Garden's design is unique among all NBA arenas. The arena was built in a circular shape and supports its ceiling with 48 steel cables instead of support beams. This means all fans in the upper deck seats have a great view of the court.

The Knicks played to a sold-out Madison Square Garden for many years. With some of the most loyal fans in the NBA, the team had a streak of 433 sellouts in a row from 1993 to 2002. It is the sixth-longest sellout streak in NBA history.

Madison Square Garden is one of the premier sports venues in the world.

Fans who visit Madison Square Garden today will see many new features. It went through a huge renovation in 2013. The arena was overhauled for three years at a cost of $1 billion. There are suites and club seating for home games and concerts. The Lexus level suites give guests exclusive benefits and the energy of lower-level seating. For upper-level seating, the signature level suites and lounges offer guests a great experience.

Madison Square Garden is an absolute must-see for any fan touring the best arenas in the NBA. Madison Square Garden is located on 33rd Street in New York between 7th and 8th Avenues. Fans wanting to get there have many transportation options. Penn Station is underground below the arena. A total of 14 subway lines reach Madison Square Garden. Four different bus lines will take fans within one block of the arena.

3 SCOTIABANK ARENA

Only one arena in the NBA has a club inside it opened by a rapper. That would be Scotiabank Arena, home of the Toronto Raptors. Canadian rapper Drake opened a club inside Scotiabank Arena. This invite-only club features leather couches and elegant chandeliers.

FUN FACT
The current site of Scotiabank Arena was previously a post office building in Toronto.

Most Raptors fans will never get to visit Sher Club. But that doesn't mean they'll miss out on luxury. The arena has 1,020 club seats and 65 executive suites for guests looking to be pampered a bit. They will also enjoy a state-of-the-art $1 million sound system installed in the arena. Those are only a few of the amenities that helped Scotiabank Arena develop a reputation as one of the best venues in professional sports.

SCOTIABANK ARENA

Toronto, Ontario, Canada

Date Opened: February 20, 1999
Capacity: 19,800
Home Team: Toronto Raptors

The Raptors are the only Canadian team in the NBA. Fans from the United States hoping to visit will need to pack their passport for the trip. Visitors at Scotiabank Arena can sample Canadian

Scotiabank Arena hosted the NBA All-Star Game in 2016.

specialties at a Raptors game. Food options include poutine, Tim Hortons coffee, fresh sushi, and more.

Fans can stay toasty when visiting Toronto and Scotiabank Arena in the winter. The arena connects to Toronto's PATH walkway system. PATH is the largest underground shopping area in the world. It connects many of Toronto's tourist attractions. Many restaurants and shops are located in the PATH.

Scotiabank Arena also added a new area called Leaf Legends Row outside the arena in 2014. The outdoor space hosts tailgating and pregame parties. A new entrance was added to the building's west end, and new concession stands and shops were also added.

FUN FACT

The Raptors' practice court is located inside Scotiabank Arena. Only 10 other NBA teams have their practice facility connected to their arena.

Scotiabank Arena has hosted many events since it opened in 1999. That includes major concerts, the NBA All-Star Game, and Toronto Rock lacrosse games. Raptors fans are hoping it won't be long before Scotiabank Arena hosts its first NBA Finals.

BANKERS LIFE FIELDHOUSE

Some NBA venues are called arenas. Some are called centers. But there is only one fieldhouse in professional basketball: Bankers Life Fieldhouse in Indianapolis.

The Indiana Pacers call Bankers Life Fieldhouse their home. A fieldhouse is typically designed to hold multiple sports. Bankers Life Fieldhouse was designed to replicate the barn-like appearance of high school and college fieldhouses in Indiana. Basketball is among the most popular sports in the state.

The unique architecture of Bankers Life Fieldhouse has received much praise. It has been called "A Cathedral to Basketball." It is considered one of the best arenas in the entire NBA. The building is made with more than 600,000 bricks. The 58,000 square feet (5,400 sq m) of glass windows provide a lot of light for the fieldhouse. Builders brought in the largest crane

BANKERS LIFE FIELDHOUSE

Indianapolis, Indiana

Date Opened: November 6, 1999
Capacity: 17,923
Home Team: Indiana Pacers

Pacers fans at Bankers Life Fieldhouse enjoy one of the best basketball experiences in the NBA.

in the world to lift parts of the building up to its highest points. It took 1,200 workers approximately two years to complete the construction.

Bankers Life Fieldhouse was the first retro-style building to be built in the NBA. But plenty of modern amenities can be found inside. Four large screens are used for the main video board. Two of the screens measure 50 by 21 feet (15 by 6 m). The other two are 25 by 14 feet (8 by 4 m). The sound system at Bankers Life Fieldhouse was also upgraded in 2012. For guests looking for a bite to eat, the arena houses a variety of concessions and restaurants on each level during games. Jason's Deli is also open year-round.

The Pacers played in the NBA Finals in 2000. That was only their first season playing at their brand-new fieldhouse. Reggie Miller and Jalen Rose helped lead Indiana to the Finals against Kobe Bryant, Shaquille O'Neal, and the Los Angeles Lakers. The Pacers won two home games in that series, but the Lakers won the championship by winning Game 6 in Los Angeles.

The venue was originally named Conseco Fieldhouse. It was changed to Bankers Life Fieldhouse in 2011. There are dedicated pick-up and drop-off locations to get guests using ride-sharing services to and from the game.

FUN FACT

Bankers Life Fieldhouse is the busiest public building in the state of Indiana. Approximately two million people attend games and concerts at the fieldhouse each year.

UNITED CENTER

It doesn't get any bigger than United Center. The home of the Chicago Bulls is the largest professional sports arena in North America. The building is a whopping 960,000 square feet (89,000 sq m). The large arena has plenty of room for fans, too. It seats nearly 21,000 fans for NBA games.

No name is bigger in Chicago than Michael Jordan. The Bulls legend began his career at Chicago Stadium. Jordan retired from basketball in 1993 to play minor league baseball. The Bulls moved into the new United Center while Jordan was retired. He came out of retirement late in the 1994–95 season. By then, the Bulls were playing in United Center.

Jordan and the Bulls were a dynasty. They won three straight championships from 1996 to 1998 while calling United Center home. Jordan led the NBA in scoring all three of those seasons. He previously helped the Bulls win three consecutive NBA championships in the old Chicago Stadium in 1991, 1992, and 1993.

UNITED CENTER

Chicago, Illinois

Date Opened: August 18, 1994
Capacity: 20,917
Home Team: Chicago Bulls

16
4:06
1
20
BULLS
VIDANTA RESORTS
THEATER BOXES
ATLANTA
CHICAGO
BULLS
1
20
ZTE
KIA
KIA
KIA

The success at the old arena carried over to the new one. The United Center is called the house that Michael Jordan built, and the streak of championship teams that played there helped cement his legacy.

Chicago clinched two of its NBA titles at United Center. The Bulls beat the Seattle SuperSonics at home in Game 6 of the 1996 NBA Finals for their fourth championship. Chicago won another title at United Center one year later. Jordan and the Bulls topped the Utah Jazz in Game 6 in Chicago in 1997.

FUN FACT

Chicago Bulls fans got used to winning at the United Center. Jordan and the Bulls posted a 39–2 home record during their 1995–96 championship season.

Fans visiting United Center today will see tributes to Jordan and other Bulls greats around the arena. A 12-foot (4-m) statue of Jordan greets visitors inside of United Center. The Jordan statue is now located inside a new atrium that was added to United Center in 2017. The atrium is open on days when no game is being played. That means fans can come see the Jordan statue without attending a Bulls game.

Bulls fans have witnessed a lot of great basketball from players such as Michael Jordan and Derrick Rose.

FUN FACT

The first event ever in the United Center was not a basketball or hockey game. Instead, it was a professional wrestling match. The World Wrestling Federation held SummerSlam at the United Center on August 29, 1994. The arena was reconfigured to seat 23,000 fans for the event.

The addition also includes a 10,000-square-foot (900-sq-m) team store. Fans can buy Bulls gear and do other activities there. Visitors can try being a sportscaster and call a Bulls game. A photo booth and interactive screens help add to the experience. The renovations also pay tribute to their old stadium. The Chicago Stadium Club is located on the second level of the arena. It even boasts an exclusive restaurant, Chef's Table.

The United Center boasts a statue of Jordan, remembering his six championships for the Bulls.

UNITED
MICHAEL JORDAN

6 AMERICAN AIRLINES CENTER

It's not easy to make the outside of an NBA arena stand out. The architects who built American Airlines Center in Dallas certainly did. The exterior of the building features brick, granite, and limestone. The curved roof alone used more than one million bricks. Its dramatic arches at each of the building's four entrances welcome fans to the arena.

FUN FACT

The Mavericks and Stars occasionally play games in American Airlines Center in the same day. The arena can be converted from one sport to another in under two hours.

American Airlines Center underwent a renovation in 2017. Mavericks owner Mark Cuban wanted the team to have the most high-tech locker room. It includes facial recognition software. The program identifies a person by his or her face when they try to enter the locker room. An identified player or staff member can then be shown game notes on a screen.

AMERICAN AIRLINES CENTER

Dallas, Texas

Date Opened: July 17, 2001
Capacity: 19,200
Home Team: Dallas Mavericks

The Dallas Mavericks have a great tradition of winning at American Airlines Center.

The technology at American Airlines Center isn't only in the locker room. Fans will also notice high-tech features. In 2009 the arena became the first in the NBA with a 1080p high-definition video board display. Each of the four main screens is 30 feet (9 m) wide and 18 feet (5 m) tall.

The seating bowl of American Airlines Center has retractable seats. That makes it easy to convert it from a basketball court to a hockey rink. American Airlines Center seats 19,200 fans for Mavericks games and 18,532 fans for Dallas Stars hockey games.

American Airlines Center has hosted the NBA Finals twice. The first time was in 2006. The Mavericks lost to the Miami Heat that year. Dallas won the NBA title five years later in 2011. The Mavericks also played the Heat during that championship. Miami's arena also has the name American Airlines in it. The Heat play their home games at American Airlines Arena in Miami.

FUN FACT

Locals call the American Airlines Center "the Hangar."

The Mavericks' home arena is located in an area called Victory Park. There are many other attractions in the 72-acre area. That includes a theater, a museum, restaurants, and plenty of shops. The Victory Park area also has lots of housing options.

STAPLES CENTER

You never know who you might see attending games at Staples Center. Perhaps you'll spot famous musician Beyoncé or actor Will Ferrell. You might even see top athletes from other sports.

The stars come out to watch basketball at Staples Center in Los Angeles. Many Hollywood celebrities go to watch the Los Angeles Lakers or the Los Angeles Clippers. The teams share Staples Center. It opened in 1999. It is the only arena in the NBA that is shared by two teams. The Lakers previously played at the Forum in Inglewood, California. The Clippers moved to Staples Center from the Los Angeles Memorial Sports Arena.

FUN FACT

Staples Center actually has a different seating capacity for the Lakers and Clippers. The Clippers arrangement calls for a second row of seats around the baseline. It seats 18,997 fans for Lakers games but seats 19,060 for Clippers games.

STAPLES CENTER

Los Angeles, California

Date Opened: October 17, 1999
Capacity: 19,060
Home Teams: Los Angeles Lakers, Los Angeles Clippers

The arena has hosted many big games. The Lakers have won five NBA championships since Staples Center opened. They won three straight titles from 2000 to 2002. The Lakers clinched their title in 2000 with a win over the Indiana Pacers at Staples Center. The Lakers also won championships in 2009 and 2010. They won the 2009 title on the road but clinched the championship at home the following year, beating the Boston Celtics in Game 7 at Staples Center.

FUN FACT

The fastest Staples Center has ever been converted from a hockey venue to basketball court was one hour and 50 minutes.

One of the most memorable individual performances at Staples Center came in January 2006. Lakers Kobe Bryant put on a show against the Toronto Raptors. Bryant scored a whopping 81 points that night. It was the second-most points ever scored in an NBA game. Only Wilt Chamberlain scored more points in a game. Chamberlain had a 100-point game in 1962 with the Philadelphia Warriors.

Bryant is one of 10 players whose jersey was retired by the Lakers. He had both his No. 8 jersey from early in his career and his

No. 24 jersey retired in 2017. All 16 of the Lakers' retired numbers hang from the rafters at Staples Center.

It can be challenging hosting two team in the same arena. That is definitely the case with the Lakers and Clippers both playing at Staples Center. Each team has its own unique court. Workers must

Kobe Bryant had a huge game against the Toronto Raptors in 2006 at Staples Center.

Although the Clippers and Lakers share the Staples Center, the arena is set up differently for each team.

change the courts for each game. Even the hoops used by each team are different.

The two teams sometimes have games on the same day at Staples Center. It takes approximately an hour to change the courts between games. Things also get tricky when the arena is changed for hockey to host the NHL's Los Angeles Kings.

Staples Center is located in downtown Los Angeles. The area surrounding Staples Center is called L.A. Live. When visiting the

Staples Center, guests won't have a problem finding things to do. Restaurants, theaters, and other forms of entertainment are available in the L.A. Live area.

Some of the celebrities who come to watch Lakers or Clippers games also perform on stage at Staples Center. The arena hosts many concerts and other performances throughout the year. It's possible Beyoncé could attend a Lakers game one week and perform in the same building the next.

MODA CENTER

Brandon Roy played only six seasons in the NBA. He was an All-Star guard for three of those years with the Portland Trail Blazers. One of Roy's most memorable games was one of the last he ever played in the Moda Center.

Roy came off the bench for the Trail Blazers during the 2011 playoffs. He scored 24 vital points and helped Portland in a playoff game against the Dallas Mavericks. Portland trailed Dallas by 18 points in the fourth quarter. Roy scored 18 points in that final quarter. Thanks to his efforts, the Blazers beat the Dallas Mavericks 84–82.

At the time that game was played, the Moda Center was known as the Rose Garden. The name changed to the Moda Center in 2013. The Rose Garden was one of only four NBA arenas at that time without a corporate name.

Although there have been plenty of big games at the Moda Center, the arena has not hosted an NBA Finals. The Blazers

MODA CENTER

Portland, Oregon

Date Opened: October 12, 1995
Capacity: 19,393
Home Team: Portland Trail Blazers

last made the Finals in 1992. That was three years before their current arena opened.

The food available at the Moda Center is some of the best in the NBA. Fans can dine on sliders and tacos as well as vegetarian

Fans at Moda Center can enjoy some of the best food in the NBA during a Trail Blazers game.

options. Among the concessions are several Portland favorites. Examples are Bunk Sandwiches and ice cream from the famous Salt & Straw.

Moda Center became the first pro sports venue to become LEED gold certified. That means the building has high standards for energy use and efficiency. Leftover food from Moda Center is donated to families in need. The majority of waste from the arena avoids ending up in landfills.

FUN FACT

Moda Center can be converted to a small music venue seating between 3,000 and 6,500 people. The larger arena is made to feel small by using curtains to close off the space.

Moda Center is part of the Rose Quarter in downtown Portland. The other venues are Veterans Memorial Coliseum, Exhibit Hall, and Rose Quarter Commons. There are several hotels located within walking distance of Moda Center. The arena is also a short walk from the Willamette River. Almost one-third of fans attending events at Moda Center get there by bike or public transportation.

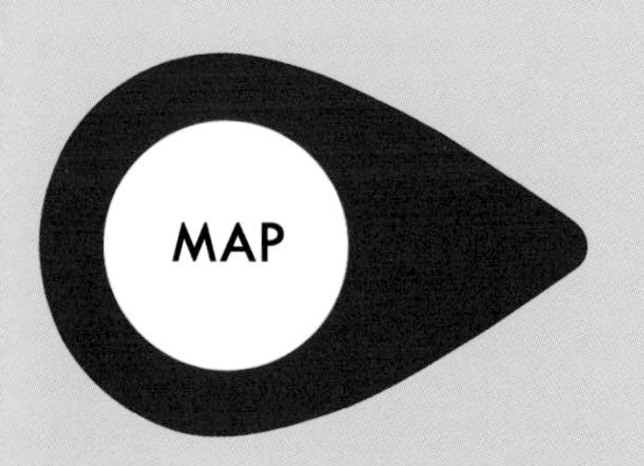

1. **TD Garden.** Boston, Massachusetts
2. **Madison Square Garden.** New York City, New York
3. **Scotiabank Arena.** Toronto, Ontario, Canada
4. **Bankers Life Fieldhouse.** Indianapolis, Indiana

5. **United Center.** Chicago, Illinois
6. **American Airlines Center.** Dallas, Texas
7. **Staples Center.** Los Angeles, California
8. **Moda Center.** Portland, Oregon

Glossary

All-Star

A player named to a team made up of the best players in his or her league.

architecture

A term to define the look or construction of a building.

dynasty

A team that dominates its league or sport for a number of years.

fieldhouse

A building enclosing a large area suitable for various forms of athletics and usually providing seats for spectators.

NBA Finals

The seven-game series that determines the champion of the NBA each year.

playoffs

A set of games played after the regular season that decides which team is the champion.

rafters

A set of beams that help hold up a roof of a building.

renovation

Restoring or updating the physical conditions of a building.

retire

To end one's career.

More Information

BOOKS

Ervin, Phil. *Total Basketball*. Minneapolis, MN: Abdo, 2017.

Silverman, Drew. *Basketball*. Minneapolis, MN: Abdo, 2012.

Smibert, Angie. *STEM in Basketball*. Minneapolis, MN: Abdo, 2018.

Online Resources

To learn more about NBA arenas, visit **abdobooklinks.com**. These links are routinely monitored and updated to provide the most current information available.

Index

About the Author

Tyler Mason studied journalism at the University of Wisconsin-Madison. He has covered professional and college sports in Minneapolis and St. Paul, Minnesota, since 2009. He currently lives in Hudson, Wisconsin, with his wife.